John Wesley Daily

The Philippine Islands, their Number, Aggregate Area and Population

John Wesley Daily

The Philippine Islands, their Number, Aggregate Area and Population

ISBN/EAN: 9783337404161

Printed in Europe, USA, Canada, Australia, Japan

Cover: Foto ©Suzi / pixelio.de

More available books at **www.hansebooks.com**

PRICE, 25 CENTS

THE

PHILIPPINE ISLANDS

Their Graphic Description by one who has lived
there — Their vast Agricultural, Mineral, and
Industrial Resources — Gold glittering in the
Sand and Gravel of every Stream — One
of the richest Gold-fields of Earth in
a land of Perpetual Summer.

How Annexation will develop the Islands rapidly
and give the United States a World-
reaching Commerce.

BY

JOHN WESLEY DAILY, A.B., M.D.

———◆———

C. C. DAILY PUBLISHING COMPANY,
BOSTON, MASS.
596 TREMONT STREET.
1898.

THE

PHILIPPINE ISLANDS,

THEIR NUMBER, AGGREGATE AREA, AND POPULATION.

ORIGIN, DISCOVERY, LOCATION, LATITUDE,
CLIMATE, SOIL, AGRICULTURAL AND
MINERAL RESOURCES.

THE PRINCIPAL INHABITANTS, THEIR CUSTOMS,
SCHOOLS, COLLEGES, AND RELIGIONS.

ANNEXATION: HOW IT WILL AMERICANIZE, CIVILIZE,
AND DEVELOP THE MANY ISLANDS, GREATLY EXTEND
OUR COMMERCE, CONSUME OUR PRODUCE, SET
OUR WHEELS A-SPINNING, AND GIVE EM-
PLOYMENT TO ALL OUR PEOPLE.

BY

JOHN WESLEY DAILY, A.B., M.D.

———————◆———————

C. C. DAILY PUBLISHING COMPANY,
BOSTON, MASS.
596 TREMONT STREET.
1898.

ROCKWELL & CHURCHILL PRESS. BOSTON.

THE
PHILIPPINE ISLANDS.

[In preparing this pamphlet for publication, the author gratefully acknowledges the assistance of Ct. M. de Moreira, professor of languages, who has lived in Manila, has travelled over and through all the principal islands of the Philippines; who is familiar with the racial peculiarities, laws, customs, and religions of the prevailing inhabitants; and who has studied the agricultural, mineral, and industrial resources of the various islands.]-

THE archipelago known as the Philippine Islands is situated in the Pacific Ocean, south-west of Japan and Korea; 500 miles south-east of China; a few hundred miles north and a little to the east of Borneo; and over 1,200 miles north of Australia.

The islands number 1,200 or more, the most of them being small and uninhabited.

The southern extremity of the group lies 5 degrees north of the equator, while the most northern boundary is 20 degrees from the equator, the latitudinal range of the islands being about as wide as that of the United States.

The Philippine Islands were discovered in 1521 by Magellan, and a few years later the Spaniards, under Villalobos, took possession of the group and named it in honor of King Philip II. of Spain, and have held it over 360 years.

The islands were again discovered on the first of last May by Admiral Dewey, who proceeded with great promptness to sink Spain's Asiatic fleet.

The aggregate area of the Philippines is 150,000 square miles, a territory equal in size to the States of New York, Indiana, Maine, New Hampshire, Vermont, Connecticut, Massachusetts, and Rhode Island.

NAMES, AREA, AND RELATIVE LOCATION OF THE PRINCIPAL ISLANDS.

Luzon, almost in the extreme north, has an area of 51,300 square miles and a population of 3,500,000 or more. Manila, the capital of the Philippines, and principal city, is situated on the south-west coast of Luzon, in latitude 14 degrees north, is a live commercial city with a population of 350,000 people, of whom about 300,000 are natives, or half-breeds of the Malay class; about 40,000 are Chinese; 7,500 Spanish;

200 Germans; 100 English; and, possibly, 100 Americans exclusive of the soldiers and sailors.

Mindanoa is the next island in size, being half as large as Luzon, and containing over 25,000 square miles. It is one of the most southern islands, intensely fertile, and capable of supporting a very dense population.

The islands lying between Mindanoa, near the equator, and Luzon, in the far north, are known as the Bissayas, the largest of which are the following:

Samar, with 13,000 square miles; Mindora, 12,800; Panay, 11,350; Leyte, 10,000; Nigros, 6,300; Masbate, 4,000; and Zebu, 2,300.

The Bissayas have an aggregate area of 60,000 square miles, being 40 per cent. in area of the entire group, and are said to have a population of nearly 4,000,000.   The total population of the Philippines in 1876, according to the best information obtainable at that time, was 6,500,000.   The "New York World's" almanac for 1898 claims for the islands a population of 9,500,000; and as this indicates an annual increase of only 2 per cent. during the last 22 years, the figures seem very reasonable.

Lying south-west of the Bissayas is a long, narrow island known as the Paragoa.   It has 8,800 square miles, being a trifle larger than the State of Massachusetts, and consists of mountain ranges, billowy highlands, gentle slopes, and beautiful valleys; is watered by numerous creeks and rivers, and is exceedingly fertile.   Here is a land of perpetual summer; the shimmering waters are alive with fish; squirrels bark and monkeys chatter from the branches of a thousand trees; the thunder-like drumming of pheasants and the warble of sweet wild birds are sounds familiar to tourists who have penetrated these tropical forests; natural beehives, replete with dripping honey, are found in the limbs and trunks of trees;

"And strange, bright birds on their airy wings
    Bear the rich hues of all glorious things;"

and yet Paragoa is no earthly paradise, for the jungles, bound together by the floating garlands of climbing plants and indigenous vines, swarm with snakes, lizards, huge spiders, tarantulas, white ants, mosquitoes, and other miserable plagues.

EARTHQUAKES.

These terror-breeding affairs are frequent and destructive in some parts of the Philippines. Manila, the capital, was almost destroyed by a shock in 1863, while another terrific earthquake visited Mindanoa in 1864, destroying most of the houses. For this reason the houses of Manila are almost all wooden structures erected with the view of withstanding whatever shocks may come in the way of earthquakes.

THE RAINY SEASON.

In many of the islands, and especially in Mindanoa, there are numerous lakes which expand during the rainy season into inland seas. The heavy rains commence in May and gradually cease about

December, the land being more or less flooded from June to November. In consequence of the heavy and frequent rains, there is scarcely any limit to the growth of vegetation, and it seems the decaying products of such wonderfully rich soil would develop malarial and pestilential conditions and cause the most malignant epidemics of fever, especially yellow fever and typhoid. But it appears that nature is exceedingly benign and considerate in dealing with many of the troublesome problems connected with life, health, and happiness, and in this case she interposes counteracting influences so as to modify the virulence of the malarial poison upon the many islands, and limit the ravages of disease.

The islands are surrounded by

the great ocean, from whose surface millions of tons of water ascend heavenward every hour during the hot season, and "as what goes up must come down," rains are frequent and copious, causing unlimited vegetable growth, and as all such growths must perish and give to earth and air the products of their decomposition, the tendency is to poison the atmosphere so as to make all the islands uninhabitable; but the same ocean that contributes to the formation of malaria, in an indirect way, permits the infected breezes that sweep over the various islands to bathe, cleanse, and purify their wings in its briny bosom. Islands, notwithstanding their natural tendencies to malarial development, are much less liable to malignant epidemics than continents, and the smaller the islands the more healthful they are, as the opportunities for laving and purifying their zephyrs in the ocean are multiplied.

VOLCANOES.

Many active volcanoes are scattered through the islands. Mayon, in the great Luzon Island, and Buhayan, in Mindanoa, have caused great devastation; and yet volcanoes are the great evolutionary forces that have operated for hundreds of centuries in raising the Philippine and Sooloo Islands out of the Pacific Ocean; they are the eruptive energies that have lifted from the deep, seething caldrons of earth the fiery lava and spread it out in vast beds upon the many islands, to be dissolved by the descending torrents of ages, and transformed into the richest soil known to man.

ORIGIN OF THE PHILIP- PINES.

Regarding the origin of these islands, there are conflicting opinions. Some authorities claim that the whole chain of the Philippines and Sooloos are simply fragments of a submerged continent. Others strongly favor the theory that they have all been raised from the depths of the ocean by volcanic eruptions; and a multiplicity of facts and observations in reference to the past and present conditions of the many islands seem to establish the truth of the volcanic theory.

We know that the planet upon which we live was once a seething mass of fire, and that it attained its present globular form when it was in a melted and liquid state. We know this because we find with our telescope millions of other heavenly bodies that are now glowing globes of liquid fire, while others are cold and dark like our earth, and give no light except the reflected rays of a sun. This teaches us the origin, life, death, and decay of worlds, and we know that every star, every glowing sun, that scintillates to-night in the infinite azure, will sometime be an immense cinder — a burned-out and blackened char.

We also know that some of the Philippine Islands are melting, as it were, with fervent heat; are constantly encroaching upon the ocean by volcanic upheavals and deposits; building mountain chains and forming broad, luxuriant beds of lava in the lower lands and valleys. Others have just completed the fiery process, are full grown, and their volcanoes have permanently ceased their eruptions.

In other islands the volcanoes have been extinct, possibly, for thousands of years. Their once violent and fiery peaks have become cold and quiet; torrents of rain have rounded them down, filled up and obliterated their craters, carried their fertilizing lava to lower levels, and all volcanic signs have disappeared. We know that all the glittering suns now thrilling their peopled systems with life and energy must in time become cold and dark. We know that hot and life-sustaining as millions of suns now are, all the dark planets of the universe once were. We know that every seething, devastating, terror-breeding volcano in the Philippines must sometime become cool and quiet.

We almost know that every green-clad island of the group that now teems with millions of life-forms and peacefully enjoys an immunity from periodic explosions was once a fire-spitting, life-destroying volcano.

THE SOIL.

The land of China is said to be the most productive and enduring upon the globe, and the fertility of the soil depends upon immense lava-beds that are a thousand feet thick in places. The soil is called *loess*, the accent being upon the first syllable, is of a dark, reddish-brown, consisting of disintegrated lava mixed with decayed vegetation.

The soil of the Philippines is almost identical in its origin, character, general fertility, and enduring properties with that of China, as the torrents of rain dissolve the lava crusts from the volcanic ranges, carrying them to the lower lands and valleys to be mixed with decayed vegetable matter.

The soil, like the *loess* of China, is of a reddish-brown, and is unsurpassed in its productive capacity.

HOW ITS FERTILITY IS MAINTAINED.

Primarily, soil, in all the countless worlds, is absolutely mineral, as it can never be mixed with animal or vegetable matter until life, growth, death, and decay are established.   Therefore the basis of all soil is and always has been mineral.

The birds that deposit millions of tons of guano upon the islands of South America, simply return to mother earth the mineral elements they obtain in the form of animal or vegetable food.

It may seem unreasonable to suppose that land can be enriched by allowing crops of vegetation to decompose upon its surface and give back to the soil only those identical elements they had extracted from it, and yet this is one of the best ways to fertilize some kinds of soil.

The mineral properties of every soil have an intrinsic tendency to sink deeper and deeper into the earth, until they reach an impervious and impassable foundation of clay or stone upon which the soil rests.

In the Philippines, where the soil is wonderfully rich in mineral ingredients, where rains are frequent and copious, where frost and snows are unknown and the season of growth is perpetual, the plants and grasses extract the mineral elements from the deep soil and deposit them upon the surface in the form of vegetable mould. In addition to this, various mineral deposits are leached from the volcanic ranges every year by floods of rain and washed to lower levels, keeping the lands constantly enriched.

CLIMATE.

From the first of November to the first of May the Philippines are almost a paradise so far as temperature is concerned, but by May first the heat begins to be oppressive, the air becomes intensely humid, and the rainy season commences. Almost every one is familiar with the fact that evaporation consumes heat. If water is spread out upon any body, it not only cools the surface of that body, but rapidly cools the air in contact with it. But for the rainy season, which lasts five or six months, the temperature of the Philippines would be unendurable from May until December, but the rains are widespread, floods of water are poured down upon the surface, and the air is comparatively cool until it commences to get dry, when, usually, another flood of rain falls, and in this way the heat of a Philippine summer, which would otherwise be extreme, is avoided.

TIMBER.

" Immense forests spread over the Philippine Islands, clothing the mountains to their summits ; ebony, iron-wood, cedar, span-wood, gum-trees, etc., being laced together and garlanded by bush-rope or palasan, which attains a length of several hundred feet. The variety of fruit-trees is great, including the orange, citron, bread-fruit, mango, cocoa-nut, guave, tamarind, rose-apple, etc. ; other important products of the vegetable kingdom being the banana, plantain, pine-apple, sugar-cane, tobacco, cotton, indigo, coffee, cocoa, cinnamon, vanilla, ginger, pepper, etc., with rice, wheat, corn, and various other cereals." (Chambers' Encyclopædia.)

GOLD IN THE ISLANDS.

Gold is found in the river-beds, and in the detritus or sediments of various mountain streams, the gold dust thus obtained being used as a medium of exchange on some of the islands, especially in the large southern island, Mindanoa. According to the best information obtainable, no decided effort has ever been made to find and develop gold mines.

It is probable that all the gold that has ever been found upon the earth has been brought to the surface by volcanic eruptions, although it is often found in the banks and beds of streams hundreds of miles from mountain ranges.

There are several interesting points in connection with gold deposits, and those of other heavy and precious metals, that may be considered to advantage here. We know that gold is a very heavy metal, that its specific gravity is 19 or a trifle more, or, in other words, it is 19 times as heavy as an equal bulk of water. We also know that platinum and iridium are 22 times as heavy as water, and that all of these wonderfully heavy metals are scarce upon the earth's surface, and are found only in mountain ranges, all of which were primarily volcanoes, or in the detrital deposits of mountain streams.

Why is this so? The answer seems easy. The globe was once in a melted condition, and, naturally enough, the intensely heavy metals sank deeply into the liquid earth.

After the lapse of ages the earth became sufficiently cool to form a crust upon its surface that was impervious to steam. Terrific volcanoes were numerous, breaking through the crust and building mountain ranges by upheavals and deposits of melted matter. It was during these eruptions that some of the heavy and very precious metals were thrown out and strewn over the sides of mountains. It was during these natural explosions that lava, containing gold, filled many of the volcanic craters and formed what we now call "veins of gold-bearing ore." As the Philippines are all volcanic formations, all raised from the bed of the ocean by eruptions and deposits, there is every reason to believe that gold exists in most of the islands, and that enterprising Americans may find a new Eldorado, a new Klondike, in that archipelago; and what a heavenly place it will be for mining as compared with Alaska!

The historical facts and conditions favoring the belief that the Philippines are among the very richest gold regions upon the earth are the following:

First, These islands are unquestionably volcanic formations, and as all gold has been brought to the earth's surface by volcanic eruptions, it is reasonable to suppose that vast quantities have been deposited in the many mountains of the Philippines in this way.

Second, It is widely claimed that the sand and gravel of all the streams of the many islands pan out gold.

Third, The gold industry, crude as it always has been, is as old as the history of the islands, and the shining metal was exported to China before the discovery of the archipelago by Magellan nearly four hundred years ago.

Fourth, The natives, uneducated and uncivilized as they are, have obtained gold for centuries from the creek and river sands, and have been using it among themselves constantly as a medium of exchange.

Fifth, The people upon the islands are not sufficiently intelligent and enterprising to find and develop gold mines, and therefore have obtained only such gold as they could find and save in an easy and simple way.

Sixth, The show of gold in the sedimentary deposits of every valley, and in the detritus of every river, creek, and brook, leads one to regard the whole Philippine archipelago as an immense cluster of gold mines.

STAPLE PRODUCTS OF THE SOIL.

There are no richer lands in the world than those of the Philippine Islands, and therefore it is not strange that such soil-exhausting staples as hemp, tobacco, cotton, coffee, sugar, rice, wheat, and corn are raised in abundance upon the principal islands.

On the broad tablelands, long slopes, and rich valleys, immense quantities of hemp are produced every year, the annual amount exported being about a hundred and thirty million pounds.

In 1890 sixteen million pounds of tobacco and one hundred and ten million cigars were exported from the islands.

Great quantities of cotton, sugar, coffee, rice, wheat, and corn are produced annually, their production affording profitable employment to hundreds of thousands, and adding in that way to the general prosperity of the many islands.

MINERALS.

The archipelago is rich in various minerals, such as iron, copper, coal, vermilion, quicksilver, sulphur, nitre, etc. Beds of bituminous coal suitable for smelting and all manufacturing purposes have been found upon several of the islands, and the amount of the "black diamond" easily obtained will afford ample facilities in the way of fuel for reducing and utilizing the many metallic ores with which the Philippines abound.

WILD BEASTS.

If wild, ferocious animals ever existed upon these islands, they have been exterminated by the inhabitants, as none are found upon any of them now.

The domestic animals are about the same as those of our own country, excepting the peculiar breeds of horses, hogs, and cattle.

SCHOOLS AND COLLEGES.

Since the discovery of the Philippine archipelago by Magellan 377 years ago the lamp of reason has been burning upon the various islands with a lurid and flickering light, and it is to be deplored that most of the people are mentally as obtuse, stupid, and superstitious as were the followers of Moses in the woods of Sinai thousands of years ago. Even in and about the cities and trading centres of the many habitable islands, the few schools that are kept up are very poorly attended. In Manila there are many schools for both sexes, but the attendance is very poor. The sexes are divided in the schools, one school being for males and another for females, and this affords further evidence of the backward condition of the people in matters of education. There are, however, some good schools, as the Saint Thomas and the Municipal Atheneum of San Juan de Latran are very important and well attended. There are also universities where the usual branches of science are taught.

WAGON ROADS AND RAILROADS.

Common roads have been established, so that the one thousand and fifty-five different villages, or *pueblos*, can have easy communication with each other, but there is only one railroad in the Philippines, and that extends from Manila to Dagapan, a distance of 196 kilometres, or about 122 miles.

There are many steamship companies that carry passengers and freight to every port of the islands, and also to America, China, and Japan.

CAUSES OF THE INSUR-RECTION.

In dealing with disease, one of the most important things to consider is the *cause* of the derangement, and there are usually two causes — predisposing and exciting. For example: A hereditary tendency to rheumatism is a predisposing cause of the disease, while an exposure to wet and cold is an exciting cause. In the war of the Rebellion, slavery was the predisposing cause, while the election of Lincoln was the exciting cause.

The opposition of Freemasonry to the prevailing religion of Brazil was the predisposing cause of the revolution in 1889, while the agitation and discussion of other questions became the exciting cause of the war that resulted in the overthrow of the empire.

In the war of the Philippines there was undoubtedly a feeling of hatred toward the Spanish government that rankled in the bosoms of many, and was to some extent a predisposing cause of the insurrection, but the most active, widespread, and exciting cause was a factional strife between Freemasonry and Catholicism, and it is probable that General Aguinaldo and other insurgent leaders "have travelled" and in one sense at least do business "on the square," their chief desire being to bring Spain from a living perpendicular to a dead level.

WHY GOLD MINES AND OTHER RESOURCES HAVE NEVER BEEN DEVELOPED.

For nearly four centuries the people of the Philippines have been degraded, insulted, robbed, and wronged; their ambition and hopes have been crushed; their education, civilization, and progress have been retarded; the Spanish government has been a vampire at their vitals, sucking the blood of honest toil; each wind sweeping over the archipelago has caught up the sighs of broken and bleeding hearts; the sands of every island have been steeped in tears wrung out by Spanish cruelty and greed; the richest and most productive lands upon which the sun has ever shone have been stirred by wooden plows drawn by time-wasting oxen; crops have been cultivated with sticks and human fingers instead of suitable hoes; sugar-cane has been beaten with sticks and stones instead of being crushed by a mill; gold has been panned from the sand and gravel of almost every river, creek, and murmuring brook that reaches the Pacific Ocean from the Philippines, and yet those people, like a pig feasting upon acorns under the branches of a spreading oak, have never raised their poor, stupid eyes to see where the gold comes from. Every tiny bee replete with the sweets of flowers points, by its course through the trackless woods, to its forest home; every grain of gold glittering in the sands of a Philippine stream points upward along the winding course of that stream to its primitive home in or about some volcanic peak, and tells, as it were, that it was once thrown from the fiery depths of the globe by volcanic explosions; that it was mixed with millions of tons of melted matter that finally cooled and hardened into stone; that it is merely a shining fragment of some rich, golc.-bearing stratum of rock from the face of which it has been ground by the erosions of a mountain stream.

The bee is unerring in directing the sportsman to its natural hive in the trunk or limb of a tree : the sparkling grains of gold strewn along the banks and beds of streams are unerring in directing the intelligent explorer to the mine from which they came.

DO WE WANT THE PHILIPPINES?

Yes, we want the whole archipelago; want the 1,400 islands whose wave-washed sands sparkle with gold; we want for ourselves and generations unborn what seem to be the richest gold-fields of the globe; we want to extend and enlarge our dominions, amplify our commerce, and carry the burning torch of reason and civilization into the darkest parts of the planet.

Evolution, life, and growth are the ruling principles of every nation until decadence and death begin. We want a country so great in extent, so vast and varied in its resources, and so world-reaching in its commerce that local failures in crops can never affect us in a serious way.

THE NEW COMMERCIAL ERA.

" This country is on the eve of an enormous extension of its foreign commerce.

" Not only does a great trade await us in Cuba and Porto Rico, — to secure which ships are already sailing from all our Atlantic and Gulf ports, — but ten new lines of steamers have been organized to trade with the Orient, and now an eleventh is announced from San Diego, Cal.

" These lines will sail some of them from the eastern and some of them from the western coasts. They will trade with Hawaii, China, Japan, South Africa, New Zealand,

Australia, Manila, the East Indies, and the Polynesian groups.

" Manila, in our hands, promises to become a rival of Hongkong in world-covering commerce.

" What and how much all this means for the American people it is not easy to estimate. The peoples with whom we are thus establishing relations want our grain, our hogs, our beef, our mutton, our agricultural machinery and implements, our coal oil, our sewing-machines, type-writers, bicycles, cutlery, crockery, glassware, toys, dolls, calicoes, silks, blankets, and, in brief, everything that the American people produce.

" This trade will enrich our merchants and ship-owners. It will set all our wheels a-spinning. It will give employment to all our people.

" The period of American home-market seclusion is past. The era of world traffic is beginning." — New York World.

LET US KEEP ALL THE ISLANDS WE CAN GET, INCLUDING THE PHILIPPINES.

We have the greatest and best country on earth. Our vast domain, with its rich limestone soil, its unlimited natural resources, temperate and diversified climate, is capable of producing the highest order of beings, mentally and physically, that inhabit the planet. In consequence of our highly favorable location geographically, and of our immense size, being as large as all Europe, we can produce enough brawn and brain and blood and bone to people not only an empire, but a world; and why not establish and perpetuate a high type of civilization upon all the islands of the earth to which we can extend our fostering and sheltering care?

Thirty centuries ago it was truly said : " Israel, thou hast slain thyself."   The same may be said of Spain, and about all of her foreign possessions have dropped into the lap of Uncle Sam like so much ripe fruit.   Why should we give them up ?   It may be a hundred centuries before another country, with more territorial possessions than discretion, blows up one of our warships and affords us an opportunity to annex such a lovely group of islands by conquest.   Islands or no islands, we need a large navy,— many times larger than we have at present, —

as the best way to avoid war is to get thoroughly ready to fight. Colt was a benefactor because his death-dealing revolver did what the courts, schools, and churches could never do — broke up fighting among men.

Through the ceaseless forces of evolution we have transcended the wildest dreams of James Munroe, have thoroughly outgrown his famous doctrine, and are now fully launched upon the broad ocean of imperialism, looking for islands. We have found some rich and choice ones that are equal in their aggregate area to England, Ireland, and Scotland, and have wrested them from Spain by an honorable and righteous war of conquest, and should hold them, as a gentleman suggests, until the sun grows cold.

It would require a book instead of the space of a dozen lines in which to enumerate the probable advantages of the Philippines to the United States. Those islands are larger in area than the State of New York and all New England; have nearly as many people; are far richer and greater in agricultural resources, and lie practically upon the threshold of China and Japan. When they are annexed and Americanized their further development and civilization will be very rapid; they will be settled by enterprising Americans and Europeans; will be dominated by Anglo-Saxon blood; their population will probably double in a decade of years, and they will become a great American emporium through which to lay the products of our shops, looms, and soil in the laps of China and Japan. What are the islands worth to us? I don't know. They are priceless.

What would it be worth to establish a greater and better trade with Asia than we have ever enjoyed with Europe, thrill the whole Pacific coast with new life, and make another New York of San Francisco? Contrary to the views of the anti-expansionists, it is the great distance of those islands and their location in Asiatic waters that render them of infinite value to us. We have but little need for stepping-stones through which to reach the markets of Europe, and therefore the Philippines would doubtless be of greater commercial importance to us than the whole of Spain.

A few timid souls fear those islands will throw grave responsibilities upon the United States and subject us to the dangers of foreign wars. There is nothing in this world worth having that does not involve responsibility. The sun that rises to-morrow morning will be greeted by a new thousand miles of landscape every hour until it reaches the Pacific Ocean, and will not shine once upon a nation of cowards. The same kind of bravery, the same kind of armies and navies, that won this rich archipelago from Spain can hold and defend it forever.

www.ingramcontent.com/pod-product-compliance
Lightning Source LLC
Chambersburg PA
CBHW021437090426
42739CB00009B/1512